CATHOLIC CHARITIES OF CHENANGO COUNTY

LEARNING HOW TO KISS A FROG

Advice for those who work with
pre- and early adolescents

by

James P. Garvin

Reprinted with permission
by
Garvin Consultant Services

ACKNOWLEDGEMENTS

To my dear friend, John Lounsbury, who inspired me to see the behavior of early adolescents through the Grimm Brothers fairy tale of THE PRINCE AND THE FROG.

To my very patient and encouraging wife Jo-Ann, my three grown-up Frogs, Debijoy, Faith, Jim Jr., and my pollywog Hope.

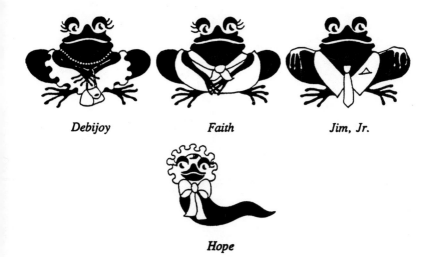

Debijoy   Faith   Jim, Jr.

Hope

LEARNING HOW TO KISS A FROG
Advice for Those Working With
Pre- and Early Adolescents

Foreward vii

Introduction ix

1. Preparing for Frogness 1

2. Becoming Frogs 9

3. Behaving as Frogs 19

4. Growing Pains 25

5. The Learning Potential of Frogs 39

6. The Stress of Being a Frog 61

Bibliography 73

About the Author 77

FOREWORD

As most of us know children are the future and without them we have none. Understanding young people has always been a major challenge for parents and teachers alike. However, in the present the process of rearing children has become a very complex endeavor.

The cultural forces with which parents and educators must contend exceed those of only a few short years ago. Values conflicts, competing conceptions of the "good life," and the scramble for economic and military security assail us daily. In such a fragmented environment we strive to provide our children with a personal, social-emotional and educational foundation that will sustain them in adulthood.

The majority of parents and educators fulfill their childrearing and educational obligations faithfully. Unfortunately, statistics suggest that too many young people "fall through the cracks" on the road to adulthood. While youngsters of all ages are susceptible to failure, early adolescents are particularly prone to "getting off track" in the process of becoming young adults.

Most readers know and understand early adolescent development and the related characteristics that identify this unique group of people. During no other time in the span of human development do individuals experience more profound developmental change in so short a timespan.

Physical, social, emotional and intellectual changes occur with rapidfire regularity.

Coupled with the dramatic shifts in everyday life the developmental changes of early adolescence challenge parents and educators to better understand early adolescents if we have any hope of supporting their successful transition from childhood to adulthood. That parents and educators need assistance in this endeavor is axiomatic.

"LEARNING HOW TO KISS A FROG" is both timely and practical. Its timeliness is obvious in that, as a guide to early adolescence, it provides an explanation of early adolescent characteristics in our educational and cultural context. It is practical in that, as a personal statement based in sound research, it provides parents with a no-nonsense explanation of the pitfalls and perils that await their early adolescents. More importantly, the publication provides concrete guidelines for parents as they confront the reality of early adolescence.

Kissing "Frogs" is a difficult though rewarding challenge for those willing to understand the dramatic forces at work in early adolescents. Skills for "coping" with the changes in young adolescents are not difficult to acquire. Parents have an excellent guide in this new publication from the Garvin Consultant Association. Read, enjoy, practice kissing "Frogs." It can be a rewarding experience!

Michael Allen
Editor
New England League of Middle Schools

INTRODUCTION

I'm sure at one time or another, everyone has read the fairy tale about the "Prince and the Frog". It's a tale of this handsome prince who had the world at his fingertips-power, influence, status, anything anyone would ever need to be happy. All of this was his for the asking, but there were certain rules of this kingdom which were not to be violated under any circumstances. A violation would mean losing all of this and instantly being turned into an ugly frog.

As the story continues, the Prince, in a moment of high temptation, violated one of these rules and was instantly turned into an "ugly frog". As a "frog", he was now relegated to swim in the dirty moat that surrounded his castle. Once a handsome prince, now an "ugly frog". The Prince knew that this "frogness" would continue forever, unless perhaps, a beautiful princess happened to kiss him, at which time he would return to a handsome Prince. So there he is, an ugly frog, feeling despondent, rejected and totally depressed because he knows that there can't be a princess anywhere who would want to kiss an "ugly frog"!

Well sure enough, about three years later this beautiful princess, from another kingdom, comes for a visit to the castle. In the course of her visit, she strolls around outside by the moat. As she sits and stares into the water, behold, this "ugly frog" leaps up on the shore! Startled at first, the princess just stares at this ugly frog, and then feeling sorry for it, she feels compelled to pick it up! Once in her hand staring at it she suddenly becomes attracted to it, and impulsively leans forward and plants a kiss on this slimy "ugly frog"! Immediately the transformation takes place and this ugly frog becomes a handsome Prince once again. They immediately fall in love and live happily ever after! What a great story and what a beautiful ending ...

After working twenty years with early adolescents, the moral of this story has been made real to me. I have concluded that perhaps the most important thing we can do for early adolescents while they are going through this stage of life, is simply to LEARN HOW TO KISS A FROG! That is what they are like! Long legs, greasy, awkward, and never seemingly knowing where they are going. Yet, over this critical period of time they are going to need adults who are willing to kiss them anyway! It is imperative for us who work with them to remember that these "frogs" are not going to be "frogs" forever. This too will pass! They are going to move out of this awkward stage and become beautiful people as long as someone is willing to kiss them while they are "frogs."

A great deal of this awkward inconsistent behavior is not the result of poor parenting or schooling, but rather from critical physical, intellectual, social and emotional development that requires difficult adjustment on the part of both adult and child. These are perhaps the most difficult years of human development, and for "frogs", an intensive period of search and separation.

As helpers, it is imperative that we work to understand and become sensitive to these characteristics. We now know so much more about early adolescent developmental characteristics than was the case ten years ago. What we know tells us, that for many kids, these years will have a profound influence toward releasing their human potential.

On the other hand, without direction, encouragement and love, it is also an easy time for "frogs" to lose hope, give up, and begin to self-destruct.

This monograph is designed to help you understand "frogs" while offering suggestions on how to go about kissing them.

PREPARING FOR "FROGNESS"

Keep in mind that as I describe "frogs" I am affectionately referring to youngsters who are somewhere between 11 and 15 years old. Not all of these "frogs" will have difficulty because we know that about thirty percent of them will not experience major problems in adjustment. They will not need to be "fussed with", nor will they bring unusual demands on our lives. They will be a delight to parents because they will be well-behaved and basically project an adult "ego ideal". These are youngsters who come from homes where parents have given them a great deal of time and attention. They feel good about themselves, having already experienced lots of success, from which they have acquired a good self-concept. These are youngsters who have already developed long-range goals and see school as a place to fulfill them. They are youngsters who are going to learn no matter where they go to school, whether it be in a middle school, a junior high school or an intermediate school. It will make little difference whether they are in a large class, small class, or grouped by ability. They just have a confidence about themselves that makes them aggressive and willing to achieve. Personal approval and attention by friends is important, but not a dominating force in their lives. Because of the other positive influences already in existence which give them the self assurance they are important, productive and worthwhile.

Our concern with these youngsters ought to be to help them refine their goals and round out the rest of their lives. We need to be careful that we don't set all of the standards of the school around them, because they are unusual and need standards especially designed for their unique needs.

Yet, we need also to develop programs which will integrate them into the rest of the school by producing cooperative learning situations with youngsters who may not be as gifted or committed to schoolwork or as self-assured. We need also to be careful not to "burn them out" with expectations and a workload that prevents them from enjoying and building the rest of their lives. We need to be careful not to see them as "just achievers" but as total people who need to be recognized and appreciated for all of their human qualities.

For the other seventy percent of these "frogs" we see a degree of changing behaviors that is not what we have come to expect at all! After all, for 11 years of parenting we worked very hard to produce a child that would respect us, listen to us and seek our wisdom in difficult situations! Then, almost without warning, a transformation takes place before our very eyes. Our loving children turn on us and leave us wondering if somehow God is getting even with us for something!

My wife and I have three children who have made it through this "frogness" stage. Our fourth is still a pollywog, and I expect that soon she will be giving us new challenges. As I reflect back to when my children first reached the age of twelve, I can remember how I thought . . . this is going to be a snap! After all, not only had I parented for twelve years but I had studied early adolescent behavior as a profession!

I simply thought it would be a matter of identifying behaviors, and applying appropriate responses! This would then produce a model child and I would obviously then be a model father! What I learned quickly, was how much easier it was working with other people's children than with my own! It's a whole different ballgame when they are your own! When I worked with other youngsters, I could leave them at 3:00 p.m., but when I go home and have my own waiting for me, that is a different case entirely! My children were masters in knowing how to strip away all of my professional armor! I'd get angry, shout, and say things I knew darn well I shouldn't. Yes, I had the book knowledge, but what I hadn't accounted for was my MENTAL HEALTH!

Some early adolescents are skilled enough to eat away at our "frustration toleration" level so quickly that regardless of how calm and collected we might think we are, we can lose it, and find ourselves doing things unbecoming of a rational human being. To compound the problem, about 30% of the parents of youngsters 11 to 15 years old have parents between the ages of 38 and 48, many of whom are going through the mid-life crisis themselves! They are at that time of life when they begin reviewing their own lives and questioning whether or not they made the right decisions in life? They often look at their "frogs" and envy their energy, and opportunity to have new options. Some of these parents don't have the frustration toleration to control themselves, much less to kiss "frogs". These parents need lots of support both at home and in the school if they are to have the sensitivity and patience to tolerate their children's behavior.

Once my children reached age 12 or so, I noticed several new behaviors that affected my ego. After all, life was pretty predictable through the first 11 years and my ego needs for love, affection, attention, self-esteem and belongingness were quite well-satisfied by my children. At about age 12 these nice ego strokes started to vanish. For example, once they reached the age of 11 or so, I remember when they came home from school they would no longer tell me about their day!

During elementary school days it was such a good secure feeling to have them come home and volunteer information about everything that happened to them over the day! I was their "confidant" and it make me feel so good to not only have the information, but to know that they liked sharing it with me! They would come bursting into the house after school to tell us all about their teachers, friends, activities, and games they played during the day, and even ask me for advice once in awhile! No question about it, I was made to feel that I was indeed one of the most important people in their lives!

What a great feeling to know that they thought enough of me to inform me of problems and tell me about important events in their lives! I felt needed and more importantly it reinforced the notion that I was a parent. Once they reached the middle school, all of this started to change. Little by little they started to shut me out of their world and my ego just didn't understand why the strokes were gone! They would now come home, maybe say "hello!", head for the refrigerator, tank up with food and scurry off to their bedrooms! Ever ask why they spend so much time in their bedrooms?

Not too long ago I had a parent ask me, "Dr. Garvin why do they spend so much time in the bedroom?" One parent remarked . . "the last time I saw my son was when he was 12, that was when he last entered his bedroom, ... I think he's 14 now . . . We pass notes under the door once in a while, . . . what's going on in that room? Before you finish reading this book perhaps you will see why this room is so important to "frogs".

When all of this started, my nervous system wasn't prepared for what was about to happen! Why were my children all of a sudden shutting me our of their lives? I became so frustrated I started to misread situations, thinking that the reason they were shutting me out was because they were doing things they wanted to hide from me! (This often happens to parents when "frogs" shut them out. They become suspicious.) I even started to pry! The more I pried, the more they shut me out!

Don't be alarmed by all of this when it happens, it's just that "Frogs" will see parents differently now, because they need to develop a private life and it isn't "cool" to depend on adults as confidants as they did when they were children. My "frogs" no longer needed this close confidant relationship, but as they shut me out, my nervous system kept saying, Don't let them change!" I desired to keep situations as they were, and this often created conflict and kept me from seeing things objectively. After all, what did their friends do to deserve to take my place?

Another change that occurred which affected my ego, was that they no longer wanted or need those nice "hugs and kisses"! Wasn't it great to spontaneously give and get those tight hugs when they were children? What a super feeling to have our kids run up and swing their arms around us and tell us how much they loved and missed us over the day! What a great shot to our egos!

Well, be prepared, for about the age of 12 this too will change! They won't see it as very necessary anymore. As a matter of fact I remember that after age 12 or so, I had to begin calculating when it would be appropriate to hug and kiss them without embarrassment! Some of the time it would be greeted with a "yuck!, others with an "Oh Dad!" response, or maybe if it was a good day I'd get a half hug in return. One of the things I learned quickly was not to hug or kiss them when their friends were around! This was the kiss of death!

My, how their behavior changes when friends are around! They can be warm as toast one minute, only to have a friend show up and suddenly totally ignore us as if we didn't exist! They might even turn on us just to show their friends that they are "in control" of their parents! This is part of working out the new independent-dependent conflict which we will talk about later.

Once again, all of this might be well and good for them, but what about my needs? I still want the hugs and kisses! After all, what did I do to deserve this? It is at this point where many parents don't understand, feel rejected, are offended because their need systems tell them that they are no longer appreciated. Some retaliate by developing a "bonus love" that is given only when our child begs for it!

There is really nothing wrong, our "frogs" are just moving to a larger world, with more friends who have different expectations which will demand that they shed the "kid stuff" and in their world that means showing they can be independent from all of the "mushy stuff". Parents need to know that although the outward display of physical attention will diminish, it is still a very important symbol of security in our youngsters' lives and we need to find"safe times" to reinforce this relationship. This time of life often produces moments of hurt and despair and disappointment which provide ideal opportunities for comfort. We just need to be patient and look for the right time. The right time will often be when they are alone.

Soon you will discover that they no longer want to do all of those nice neat family things you were so accustomed to over the earlier years! We have a small campsite on a lake in Maine. I can remember how much my children used to look forward to the weekends when "as a family" we would motor to the lake and enjoy the swimming, skiing, and sailing. They would start packing for the trip on Wednesdays and be in the car ready to go when I came home from work on Fridays!

Wow . . . how exciting it was to see the family doing things together! Everything started to change once they entered the junior high days . . Around 12 years of age it was like pulling teeth to get them to go at all ! They always had excuses as to why they couldn't go. Either a friend wanted them to visit, or there was football game to see or a special school event going on, or something. I soon found out that the only way to get them to go was to promise that they could bring a friend! Once we arrived at the lake they would go off by themselves and we wouldn't see them until we went looking for them when it was time to return! Once again, my needs system wanted them to continue to swim, sail, fish and ski with me!

Sometimes it's harder for parents to let go than it is for children. It is hard to envision them as anything more than children. It is hard for us to tell our need system that we can now make the adjustments of learning to live more on faith without tangible evidence. The transition from childhood to adolescence is a shaky time for our children but in many cases the transition is every bit as difficult for parents.

Yet our children must learn to search and separate and many times it requires doing it without Mom and Dad. There is no other way to do it if our children are to move from dependency to the type of independent behavior necessary to take control and be responsible for their own lives.

This process begins when they are "frogs" and as parents or teachers or in whatever helper role we may find ourselves, we must take care not to hang on to them just to satisfy our needs. Just as they need to grow, so too do we. Just as they find new ways of satisfying needs so too do we need to find new ways to relate to them. In the process we need to find new supports so we are both free to grow and be more effective.

BECOMING FROGS

How do our children become "frogs"? What happens to them that brings about this strange transformation? Let me attempt to describe it for you by using an analogy.

I want you to envision a dock, stretching out over a lake. At the end of this dock the water is 20 feet deep. Attached to the end of this dock is a large boat and way off in the distance at the other end of the lake is an island, that we will call "High School".

Using this analogy, most developmentalists would say that the dock is like the first 11 years of life. It represents a support system designed to give whoever uses it, confidence that it will hold them up safely. You might not be able to swim at all, but if you have confidence in the construction of this dock, you could walk out to the end and have your nervous system completely relaxed! All you need to do, is trust that whoever built the supports, did it right.

You might even get to the end of this dock with your nervous system so relaxed, you feel the freedom to gaze out into the horizon and absorb everything you see. You might even lean over the edge of the dock and stare into the water, being even more reminded that you are over deep water, and still be completely relaxed, simply because you have come to put your faith and trust in the supports holding you up.

Over the first 12 years of life, parents spend a great deal of time building similar supports into children's lives. The first three years, represented by the first part of this dock, we build support through physical closeness. Over these formative years our children are unable to converse with us, so, when they hurt we respond by picking them up and holding them, hoping to use physical means to transfer our message that we care and everything is all right. The nice part about it, is that both mothers and fathers do this spontaneously, whereas later, we will be more concerned about appearance or how others will read it.

Between the ages of three and six, as we move further out over this dock, our children begin to be invited away from home for the first time. We now develop our checklist before letting them go anywhere, to insure that these supports continue wherever they wander. We want to know where they are going, who's going to be in charge, how they are going to get there and back, what they are going to eat, what clothes they need, and after all, who is going to give them their medicine?

At the age of six, parents are asked to make a completely different kind of decision, which really demands an act of deep faith. After having control of our children's activities for six years, we are now required by law to put our children on a school bus and send them off to a place where they will be directly influenced by adults we know very little about! Think about that for a minute.

We assume that whoever the teacher is at the end of the ride, he/she will continue what we have started! We have little choice in the matter. Whoever that person is, good or bad, we have little to say about it. We simply must let them go and relinquish some of the control we have had as parents over the formative years. Obviously, most of these teachers will be wonderful people and our children will grow to love them; but for the most part, when we place our children on that bus for the first time, it is merely an assumption.

We do lots of shadow studies looking at people's behavior without them knowing it. In one of these studies we watched parents who were at the bus stop with their children for the first day of school. Remember what that was like? On the first school day you will see as many parents at the school bus stop as children!

There they are, anxiously giving last-minute instructions to their children before handing them over to the school system. Most of these parents arrive at the stop 30 minutes early to calm their children, when in reality the children are fine and looking forward to school. It is the parents who are uneasy!

When the school bus finally arrives the driver will probably be a "nice" person. (One of these days I want to do a study of school bus drivers!) No offense to those who might be reading this and are bus drivers, but some of them are strange people!

Years ago in our neighborhood, I remember watching the "frogs" assemble at the end of our driveway every school day at 7:30 a.m. to wait for the school bus. I would often sit and watch them as the girls gathered at one end huddled closely together, brushing their hair and giggling at the boys who were on the other end of the driveway, pushing and shoving and throwing things at each other. They all had these bags which housed their life possessions.

Our stop was eighth along the route, so, when the bus arrived it was almost full of "frogs". Consequently, often the driver was aggravated and angry when he pulled into our driveway. I remember watching him as he swung open his bus doors and barked orders to these "frogs" about how they were to line up and board the bus. Even after he closed the doors I could still hear his muffled voice as he worked to get these "frogs" seated. He would then back up over my lawn, and head for school to rid his bus of troublesome"frogs".

Interestingly enough, about two hours later this same bus driver would return to our neighborhood to pick up the children who had assembled at the end of our driveway on their way to elementary school. Keep in mind that we are still the eighth stop on the route. This time when he arrives the bus is full of children, but the driver now has a big smile on his face! It's almost as if he had a conversion experience somewhere between the time he dropped off the "frogs" and started picking up children.

Now he is a nice person and once he arrived, he would literally go out of his seat to greet these children! He would even call them by name! Imagine that . . he knew them by name! The children loved him! They called him "Mr. Bus Driver". They would bring him special gifts and even reach over to give him a quick hug on occasion. What a transformation! The driver loved every minute of it! Now he has children on board who like him! Children who respect what he does, children who let him be paternal, nothing like those "frogs" who make life miserable for everyone! So, on they go in this nice bus environment to the elementary school.

Once in the elementary school, the nice adult support continues all day long. It is not at all unusual to see elementary teachers walking around these schools all day long with one child under each arm. No one has to tell elementary teachers that it is all right to put their arms around children . They know that it is a necessary part of their job! They must go home at night with their arms exhausted from holding them around kids all day!

In elementary schools you won't see teachers grabbing kids and shouting or asking for passes or embarrassing them in front of others. These teachers know that these things do not work and that children need encouragement and comfort as they work. The relationship between these teachers and children becomes one of trust and confidence.

Even when these children leave school and come home, the good feelings of support might very well be continued. I don't know if your children are anything like mine, but I can still remember almost every day when they came off the school bus hauling something they made.

I would often come home from work and find a project on the dining room table and literally go through dramatics in making sure I showed my appreciation for their work. I would say, "Okay, who made this project"? My daughter, Debi, would answer, "I did Daddy!" I would then look at it and say, "Nah, you couldn't have made this by yourself". She would say, "Yes I did Daddy, yes I did!" I'd continue, "Are you sure you did this all by yourself?" "Yes Daddy, I really did" Then I'd say, "It's beautiful, what is it?"

As a matter of fact after making her feel good about it, I'd hang it on the refrigerator so anyone who came into the house for the rest of the week could see it!

Even until this day my children have collections of things from these beautiful days. I really didn't care what they were bringing home because more than anything else over these early years I wanted to recognize whatever they did to help them feel good about their work in school, to build more supports in their lives.

Then, finally, for some children this support continues on to bedtime, Mom or Dad might spend some time with them, telling a story or two before sleep, to insure that before they end the day they feel comforted and settled. Please keep in mind that I am mindful of the thousands of children who are not fortunate enough to have any of these nice things because they are homeless, or abused or unable to attract adult support. But there are still many who do, and for these children life has greater possibilities because they are loved.

My point is that many children, up until about age 12 can go to bed at night and have their nervous system completely relaxed because of the many ways we spontaneously build support in their lives. They can go to bed at night and look back on the day and say, "Hey, this isn't a bad world!" After all, my bus driver loves me, my teachers love me, and my parents love me." They can go to sleep with their nervous systems relaxed, just like yours would be if you were standing on the end of that dock knowing you cannot swim but believing in the support you experienced while walking to the end.

Although these children haven't learned to navigate their own lives yet, they trust those adults who have built the supports. Many will be so relaxed in this support that the next day they will tear into their schools moving about spontaneously and enjoying every minute of it. The reason being, that they feel safe.

This works until about age 12, when our children become"frogs". Returning to our analogy, the end of this dock represents the time when they are about to leave this self-contained, child-centered school and enter the infamous middle level school. As they stand on the end of this dock and lookout, they see a boat tied to the end. This boat will represent the middle level school. It is full of "frogs" who are early adolescents. As these children stand at the end of this dock and look into the boat, they have ambivalent feelings about what they see.

We have asked about 2,000 of these youngsters who were at the end of this dock to tell us about their thoughts as they looked toward new experiences awaiting them in the boat. Some respond positively about what and how they felt. Some told us they couldn't wait to get there because they knew this new school would offer them opportunities for new exploratory activities. They liked the idea of a larger gym, shops, cheerleading, teams and more field trips. Others told us they looked forward to it because once they got there they would not longer "be in the kids' school"! This sort of response is very important because they see it as a significant sign of being accepted by friends as growing up!

Some of them will never return to visit the elementary school because they do not want to be around adults who remembered them as kids! This is one of the problems parents will experience because once these youngsters get into this new school they still have to return home where Mom and Dad saw them as kids! As a matter of fact some will still be treated as kids which drives them even further away from wanting to be around us.

Some told us that when they were at the end of this dock and looked into the boat, they had uneasy feelings about what they perceived would happen. They were concerned that this boat was so large and looked so impersonal. They wondered, once they got into the boat, would they fit? Would they belong? Would they get lost? This is extremely important for parents and teachers to understand because, above all, these youngsters do not want to get into this boat and be the object of ridicule or embarrassment.

In many ways to be an early adolescent and be different can be death! This is why gifted and talented programs are so difficult to conduct on the middle level. Some of these "frogs" would rather not perform on their level if it means being labeled by their friends. Some refuse to go to resource rooms for the same reason. If we are going to make these special programs work on the middle level we must find a way to make them the "in thing". They must feel accepted by their peers.

You can always tell "frogs" when they get out of school because they always walk in "herds"! They never walk alone unless it is absolutely necessary! To be accepted by their peers, yet not be dominated by them, is a very important task to achieve.

Another problem that will make this trip into the boat difficult is that some will have indispensable parents who will do whatever possible to protect this youngster from what they see to be the "evils of the frogs" in the boat. This is the parent who attends school board meeting to fight for a K-12 elementary school!

They might very well say to the child the first day of junior high, something like this, "The time has

16

come for you to go into this awful school."

Some of these "frogs" might hear this from elementary teachers. Some teachers are known to say to youngsters something like, "Wait until you get to the junior high school, you can't be babies up there! Wait until you get Mr. Smith for history and he locks you in the closet for misbehaving! Wait until you get Mrs. Barns for math and she makes you stand up in front of the class until you get the right answer! All this student needs is a brother or sister who has been through this school with some war stories to tell, and along with an indispensable parent this youngster could be in fear and trepidation upon entering this new school. This indispensable parent might very will say, "Now Billy, you listen to me because I know what is best for your life. Today is the day when you go to that awful school! I want you to promise me that you will stay away from Jack, because everyone knows that Jack is on drugs! As a matter of fact most of the kids are on drugs, so stay away from most of them! Stay away from Marge and Frank because they are doing something you are too young to know about; but if you see anyone who looks like they might be doing what you think they might be doing, stay away from them! Stay away from Frank because everyone knows he hides beer in his lunch case and sells it at lunch! I had a talk with the bus driver the other day and he told me that he would save you a seat right behind him and you are to sit there everyday. If any one calls you names or picks on you, tell the driver right away and he will tell me and together we will correct the problem for you. Maybe the best thing for me to do, is drive you to school. That way I can be sure you will get there safely"!!

17

This child will be totally lost in this new school. Over the first three weeks he will throw up, have headaches, cry, all just to get to a telephone so he can call home and rescued. And sure enough, some of these indispensable parents will drive to school, pull the youngster out, and be in the principal's office the next day complaining about the awful behavior in this school. In reality the problem is not the school. It is simply that we have a delicate "frog" who is not ready to make the transition to this new stage of life.

If youngsters are going to be prepared to make this transition from the dock (elementary school) to the boat (middle level school) comfortably, they had better come off this dock having already made independent decisions, and having already been taught guidelines and values from which to make difficult decisions; having already spent time away from home, and, with a positive outlook about going to this new school. This new life of being a "frog" will not be easy and it is here where the kissing will be difficult. The success of these next few years will be more dependent on what we have established in this youngster's life while he was on the dock, than on the uncertainties of what lies ahead in the boat.

BEHAVING AS FROGS

Once in the boat these "frogs" are going to be obsessed with trying to get an answer to one basic question, that is, "NOW THAT I'M IN THE BOAT, HOW CAN I IMPRESS MY FRIENDS?" No question about it, the more you look into studies about early adolescent behavior the more you see that between the ages of 11 to 15, one of the strongest determinants of human behavior is peer influence. These "frogs" are going to be influenced more by other "frogs" on a day by day basis than by perhaps anyone else in their social lives!

David Ellkind writes about the characteristics of "frogs" and describes this period as a time when they enter INTENSE EGOCENTRISM. All of a sudden they become centered on themselves. They begin to play to an "imaginary world". Every morning they will spend 20 minutes in front of the mirror getting themselves ready. As parents we need to remember that they are not getting themselves ready for us. No . . .they are getting ready for their imaginary audience. Once they enter school they will be certain that they will be center stage and everyone else will be focused on them!

Whenever they talk to us, they won't even look at us if a mirror is close by, or even if a window is nearby. They will invariably look right by us at whatever might project an image of themselves. They enter into this stage of narcissism that is coupled with egocentrism which insists on them admiring themselves whenever possible.

If you want to see what this imaginary world looks like, take a minute to look in their bedrooms! Everything in the room reflects their imaginary world. Parents are not invited into this room, younger brothers and sisters better not enter this room, but whenever a friend comes to visit, where is the first place they take them? Yes! Right up to the bedroom so both can continue in this imaginary world. They put the posters of their personal fable heros up on the wall, have the stereo going full blast, and together they play as active participants in this world.

They will envision themselves as indestructible, immortal human beings. Because we try to bring them back to reality it is often hard to carry on a long conversation. They don't want to deal with the real world. It doesn't quite work as nicely as the imaginary one. Consequences are not part of this world which makes the parent role as a disciplinarian even more difficult. They will seldom see problems that might lie ahead as a consequence of present behavior.

We hope these "frogs" eventually move out of this stage. Perhaps at the age of 15 or so, they might find themselves asking a different question in the boat. Not "Hey . . .how do I get everyone to notice me?, but, rather, HEY . . . ANYONE KNOW WHERE THIS BOAT IS GOING?"

For about three years or so while in this transition period, most of these kids will care less where this boat is going, or if it is in danger, or how many miles it is from shore, or whether or not it is overloaded or where it is heading. They will be so preoccupied with each other, so relationship-orientated that the rest of the world will seem dull and unimportant!

Until our "frogs" ask the question, "Where is this boat going," most of what is taught in school or at home will not be viewed as a means to an end. This question, when answered, gives direction from which commitment to goals is derived. Self discipline does not develop until it is preceded by commitment. Until "frogs" are willing to commit themselves to goals, they will need to be trapped into learning and will make life miserable for many of those who are in the business of teaching.

Some people think that "frogs" ought to be committed! (I don't mean incarcerated!) Seriously, there are those who think these youngsters should show long-range commitment over these years, In my experience, I have seldom seen "frogs" take long periods of time to get organized, much less to draw up long-term goals!

Notice their conversations when talking to their friends over the telephone. They seldom say, "Mary, this is Alice, tonight, even though we are only 12 years old, we are going to dispense with our regular conversation and talk about long-range goals! Let's see if we can draw some priorities for our life! Get your paper and pencil out and let us try to structure our lives for the future!" No, not too many "frogs" talk like that. Here is what you might hear: " Mary, this is Alice. What are you going to wear to school tomorrow? Think Billy really likes me? What a jerk I made of myself today, think anyone saw it? Come on over and see the new poster in my bedroom. How about the latest record? Did you watch MTV yesterday? Got tickets to the next rock concert?

When you listen to what "frogs" talk about most, you will find that it is about early adolescents! It is about what is going on in their world right now. They are wise enough to know that few adults like early adolescent lifestyles, because they don't fit the adult ego ideal! Adults want them to begin thinking about college, jobs, a cancer cure, paying bills and being responsible. This is why they have such solidarity with each other, why they block us out of their lives at times. They know everyone wants them to "grow up" and become serious about life! To them, the present is all that counts.

This egocentrism is very important to understand when trying to help our "frogs". Roughly between the ages of 11-14, to them, the future is not going to appear real or important. You find yourself saying until you're blue in the face, "You better study now if you're going to be ready for high school!" (high school teachers will shout loudest in this regard), or, "This is a cruel world and you better grow up soon if your going to survive"!

"Frogs" are not for the most part future thinkers! This egocentrism does not make them sympathetic to problems of life, nor do they care about the solutions. Try telling a 12 year-old about the hunger in India and see how sympathetically they respond! Many of them simply do not want to see adult reality. They prefer to live in the imaginary world their egocentrism demands.

They are name droppers, always going to famous places and meeting famous people, but in reality none of it is true. Over these early adolescent years it just does not work to motivate "frogs" by using the future as leverage. We need to find ways to let them be early adolescents and yet feel a sense of pride and enthusiasm in being able to regulate their lives successfully within their capabilities.

Well, while these "frogs" are floating around in this boat for three or four years, keep in mind how difficult the task might be. They are not operating on long-range goals. They will be inconsistent, loving you one day and hating you the next. They will not be structured in their life. They will not always follow through on our instruction and will use enormous energy trying to convince us that it is not at all true!

All these are characteristic of egocentrism and just think how difficult it must be for all those teachers out there who work with 120 of them each day of the school year! These people must be herculean to get these "frogs" to learn a curriculum when their very nature is so opposed to it! Very few people would ever choose to be with 120 early adolescents for 180 days as profession!

Less I have caused you to book passage to a far-off place, let me tell you that this egocentrism will not last forever. They will de-center themselves as they enter the job market to make some spending money. They will soon learn that the boss is not concerned about the imaginary world, so for the sake of making extra money, they might take objective feedback.

They will move to more intimate relationships which they soon will find won't work unless they are willing to take feedback. These and other incidents will help in this de-centering process. Perhaps most important to this process is to help our "frogs" move to that all important question, "Where is this boat going?" Once this is answered, then sacrifice and hard work might be in order.

GROWING PAINS

While our "frogs" are in the boat, several things happen to them developmentally over which they have little or no control. They must, however, choose how to cope with them and it is here where they will need our help.

We know that over these years they experience enormous body changes. Perhaps most significant of all these changes is the "growth spurt". My experience working with "frogs" tells me never to underestimate how important the body type or the "soma" type is to an early adolescent. They are self-conscious anyway, but I do not know of anything they are more self-conscious about than how they look physically!

You cannot tell how old a "frog" is by the way he looks! Go into a typical seventh grade class and look around. I bet you will see some youngsters who look like nine year-olds and some who look like 16 year-olds, yet they are all probably around 13 years of age! This might not mean that much to the reader because as an adult you have learned how to adjust to your body (for a better or worse), but to a youngster who does not fit into the ideal it could be perceived as death! Growing up to "frogs" has nothing to do with their chronological age! Believe me, they would much rather be 11 years old and look 14, than be 14 and look 11! If you question that this is unimportant in their lives, watch them when they pass from one room to the next at home; or , as they pass down the corridors in school! They are always jumping trying to reach the door frame. Once they are able to slap it they start for the ceiling!

I wish I had never painted the ceilings of my house white when my children were in this growth spurt! Once they could jump and reach the ceiling, we had finger marks everywhere! It was important for them to see that they could touch something today they couldn't reach yesterday! Especially, it is important in school where they can show their friends!

I remember that when my children thought they were going through the growth spurt they had the practice of going up to their bedrooms and measuring themselves on the side of their closet doors. I can still see them as they backed up and penciled a line from their heads followed by the placing of a date. They did this religiously every day and once this process indicated growth, we all had to run upstairs to verify that indeed, at long last, growth was taking place!

One of my children did not grow very much over these years. He looked more like an eight year-old than a 13 year-old when he entered the seventh grade. It was like pulling teeth to get him to attend school! Even more difficult, he did not want to participate in anything once he got there! His academic life hit rock bottom. For him, the critical problem centered around his perception of physical inadequacy. He simply did not feel that he was "normal" and felt psychologically unsafe.

What really bothered him was being called "a

shrimp" or avoiding areas where he knew he would be the object of ridicule (school bus, lunch room, halls, etc.). Interestingly enough, once he started to grow he gained 10 pounds and grew about 4 inches the first year. Consequently, he got more involved in school and the rest of his life settled down.

About five years ago I was in a middle level school of 2,000 students. My purpose was to do a shadow study (watching children's behavior without them knowing it). I made the mistake of being caught in the hall when the bell rang! Within seconds, 2,000 of these "frogs", all going through the growth spurt, filled the halls. For the first few seconds I thought to myself, I wonder what person ever thought it was a good idea to ring a bell six times a day and turn 2,000 early adolescents loose in a narrow corridor for a three minute period? My experience told me that you never turn large early adolescent groups loose in the same place at the same time, much less 2,000!

Oddly enough, schools have attempted to correct this problem by requiring that teachers stand watch over a problem administrators have set in motion. Research clearly shows that over half of the disciplinary problems in middle level schools occur in the halls. Anyone who knows much about "frogs" knows that you just do not put large numbers of them in the same place and turn them loose, much less in a narrow corridor! I am happy to report that many schools have corrected this problem by simply reorganizing passing time.

Anyway, to get on with my story . . . the bell rang and I watched these "frogs" as they entered the halls. The first thing the boys had to do was something physical- hit, kick, or push someone. A brief study into the endocrinology of the early adolescent boy shows that if a boy is sitting passively in a class for more than 12 minutes, he is going to come out into the hall swinging! As a matter of fact most writers indicate that the concentration level of a boy is only about 10 minutes anyway!

For this young boy there is this ongoing conversation with his body after about 10 minutes of inactivity. The body says, "Look, we are growing and we must move!" The boy responds by saying, "I can't move because the teacher said I have to sit up straight and be quiet!" The body responds, "Okay, move something!!!!"

We have clocked how often a boy moves some part of his body during these growth years. Something moves about every three seconds! As a matter of fact, if teachers do not let these kids get up and move around every 15 minutes or so, they will get a very good opportunity to test their management skills

We also looked at girls as they entered the halls. Most of them had to socialize right away. They often talked with friends but at times they just talked to anyone. On occasion they were not talking to each other but simply talking to be heard. After all, they only had three minutes to do neat things! We watched them as they bounced off each other as they walked through the halls. They looked as if they were moving in seven different directions!

The next thing they had to do was find their lockers. This was fun, because once they found them many of the kids could not open them! They were faced with this combination lock challenge! Whenever you see lockers with dents, it is not because they had a fight with their friends, it is because they had a battle with their lockers!

The problem is that while the body is going

through this growth spurt it creates a new eye-hand coordination problem. With the new muscles and tendons growing, "frogs" need time and experience to learn how to manage them. This is why they are clumsy and awkward, knocking things over, tripping over their own feet, etc.

The people who really get upset with this one are English teachers! They cannot understand why these kids lose their writing legibility skills. Well, I suggest that perhaps part of this problem might be related to a biological problem not neglect.

Once these students finally reached their next class, most of them threw their books on the desk and propelled their bodies into the chair by chance! I recently had the opportunity to watch an eighth grade class. For some reason the teacher had all the girls sitting up front and all of the boys across the back rows. After about 30 minutes, many of the girls were still sitting up fairly straight because they had attained fairly good control of their bodies, having almost completed the growth spurt. The boys (just in the middle of the growth spurt) had completely lost control of their bodies. Their bodies had unconsciously slid under their desks with chins resting on the desk top and arms flapped over each end.

I watched as one particular boy lost complete control of his body. He fell asleep and slowly fell out of his chair onto the floor with loud thud! The teacher immediately shouted, "Bill get up off that floor! You are not going to make up for lost sleep in this room!" Once Bill hit the floor and jolted his blood system he was fine, he just needed to circulate to keep his metabolism active.

Maybe Bill didn't get his sleep the night before, but unique to "frogs" is that they might very well fall asleep during an inactive period for reasons beyond their control. It is for this reason that teachers must plan classes with active rather than passive learning activities.

Once the growth spurt starts, it generally follows a general pattern. First the arms and legs grow, then the hands and feet grow. They look like miniature frogmen as they drift from one place to another. It becomes an effort to pick up their feet so they often drag them. They often cannot put one foot in front of the other without tripping. Boys with long arms often stand with one arm holding the other. Girls walk around with their arms folded (for several reasons!). Boys experience their feet growing rapidly and they all have to have "Nikes" ankle high, laced half way up.

When they walk, awkwardness causes them to lean forward looking as if they are going to fall on their faces. Some adults get all bent out of shape with these plastic-like characteristics. It is customary to hear them saying "Aren't you ever going to walk straight?" or, "Please show me that you can sit up straight for at least 10 seconds!"

Another interesting characteristic of the middle level school centers around the unique inter-social behavior attached to this growth spurt. Once in the eighth grade, girls have completed about 80% of this growth spurt. They do not want to have anything to do with boys who are "immature" and look like children! With this new physical shape they are looking to the older "more mature boys" in the high school (by the way, the older boys will welcome them if they are physically endowed!).

The eighth grade boys are not happy with being put down by these girls, so what do they do? These obnoxious activities to show off - muscle shirts, crude language, anything to impress this lady that even though he may look like a kid, he indeed has physical prowess.

This is a unique problem to middle level schools. On the elementary level the body really is not changing as rapidly. It is relatively unimportant to social recognition. On the high school level they will have battled through this growth spurt and intimate "personal" relationships will take the place of "group" attachment. During the middle years, the shape and proportion of the body could create definite social problems which often interrupt lofty preconceived teacher instructional objectives.

The "frogs" who are delayed in beginning this growth spurt might well display unusual characteristics both at home and school. At home, they are likely to assemble friends their size or smaller, which means it is not unusual for them to pick younger friends. This will enable them to feel a sense of power and control. The age difference will not be as important as the feeling of "size" security. Younger children will consider this a priviledged relationship. After all, how many get to be accepted by an older person as a special friend!

For the delayed "frog" this could prevent having to face the necessary struggles of social adjustment to early adolescent development. Moving through early adolescence requires that one learns to select and adjust to friends, without being dominated by them. The delayed youngster who selects younger friends, rather than fear domination, might compensate by dominating and using others who can be controlled. This often means a prolongation of children's games and activities rather than moving into the expected group activities commensurate with their own age.

Adolescents will struggle through this "independent-dependent" behavior to control over others. This will often be manifested in sibling rivalry, control over parents (especially when friends are around) or in selection of friends that can be controlled where "hero worship" can be attained.

In school the delayed youngster who perceives inadequacy might try to walk to school rather than ride the bus. The bus could be a place where others might make issue of his size. This is the youngster who might insist on getting a ride to school, then to remain in the car until the bell rings to avoid having to mingle with others. During school such youngsters often spend the day hiding or waiting until the last minute to leave a class in order to avoid having to encounter large groups in the hall. Events like lunch and physical activities might be very uncomfortable experiences.

In the classroom these youngsters are characterized by always nominating and voting for themselves whenever an election takes place. Whenever they are asked to do board work they will always stand on their toes to insure their work is as high on the board as possible. They might very well be absent when they are assigned an oral report. The last thing they want is to stand in front of the class and put their bodies on display!

Physical education could be the activity they will most avoid. It is in the gym where this inadequacy is put "on stage" because now the body is displayed in a uniform. Research shows clearly that kids who are latent in body growth might resist any activity where physical exposure is required and where physical competition is a requisite. It is ironic, because it is the "macho" type who is often hired to teach these classes. Because of the size and shape and variety of these"frogs", physical education people need to create activities that help them learn coordination and cooperation skills and focus less time on highly competitive activities.

Adults often treat children as they look, not according to their age. It is not at all unusual to see youngsters 13 or 14 years old who look like eight year-olds being treated as such. We tend to think they are still babies because they look so small. This delayed youngster might develop the generalization that all adults see them this way and avoid being in places where adults are in charge.

It is hard for this youngster to gain ego reinforcement from both adults and peers and frustrating because there isn't anything they can do about it until nature starts its work and the body begins to grow. To avoid a pattern of inferiority I suggest that parents work at identifying their youngsters' "special" gifts or skills and provide opportunities that will allow these gifts to magnify. If they are good at art, get them around people who are artists or if they like to build things put them in touch with others who have the same interest; this might help put the accent on mutual strengths rather than on perceived inadequacies. Once the body begins to develop youngsters will become more involved in school and feel more positive about themselves.

The precocious "frog" might also deal with inadequacy. These youngsters are perceived as able to do anything because they look older. They are usually popular, get elected to positions, and singled out for special attention. If they are physically endowed they are welcomed by the older groups which might be dangerous because the group expectations might require an emotional awareness not yet developed. This is the youngster who most likely will be "awkward" or "clumsy" and always knocking over everything.

Since the body is growing so fast and the metabolism slowing down, these youngsters might look like they're in slow motion. Understand please, that some of these "frogs" see themselves as inadequate as do the latent youngsters. Their problem is the opposite. They are embarrassed about everything growing so fast, standing so tall above others, or looking "out-of-place" with others their age. Adult expectations are higher because they "look" so much older.

School people, and others working with "frogs" in an adult capacity, need to study this problem and develop programs to accommodate these unique needs. All these things affect self-concept development at a time when this "frog" is seeking to find a workable personal identity.

Schools with good advisee/advisor programs have accommodated this by planned activities to insure for strong ego support. I find that whenever adult priorities put more pressure to achieve or compete than the youngster's adaptability to such pressures, both the academic and self-concept suffer dramatically. I remind you that if this "frog" moves into the next level of schooling with a poor self-concept chances are that the pattern of academic failure will continue. Too often this leads to less desirable habits and friends as a form of escape.

Another physical problem for these "frogs" relates to sexual development. Again, I remind you that dealing with this problem today is considerably different than it was 30 years ago! Today we have "frogs" 11-years-old going on 30! Not only are they developing earlier, but they are doing it in a world that is wide open!

Puberty has been occurring earlier and earlier now for the past 50 years or so. What we experienced at the age of 15 or 16 is now experienced by "frogs" 11 or 12 years old. Don't ever think that they are going through the same experiences we had. Today youngsters are dating at the age of 12. They have all sorts of new enticing things to do advertised regularly on MTV or other television commercials and they probably have access to more transportation than I do! They are much bolder. You see them hitch-hiking across the country, or in airports pricing cheap flights, or riding with older adolescents on mopeds or whatever.

They have opportunities to get more involved at an earlier age. More importantly, they might have the body and sexual capacities to be affected. Last year over 13,000 youngsters under 13 years of age gave birth to a child. Eight thousand of these young girls gave birth to their second child.

Accurate information on human sexuality will be hard to find. Fathers will give 8% of this information and mothers 24% Unfortunately, the rest of the information will come from their peers who themselves do not know what is happening! Now this is no different than what we went through years ago, except that today these kids have to adjust to it two or three years sooner.

They are younger and emotionally perhaps not as able to deal with it as someone who has lived two or three years longer. It is quite an eye-opening experience to visit a typical middle level school and see girls in the sixth grade with tight pants, low cut blouses, make-up and the sexiest walk you'd ever expect to see! Boys wear tight jeans and tank shirts suggesting new physical growth. Boys and girls walk around arm-in-arm. Somehow we have this idea that our "frogs" are supposed to be in the middle of this all day yet have the power to abstain until they are responsible enough to discipline themselves!

Over this time period this young girl will experience the onset of menses. For most girls this won't be a problem. Only about 20% of these girls have a problem and for the most part they are youngsters without information or with built-in fears, guilt, or a transferred feeling of pain delivered by a mother who has considered it her "curse" in life. However, for some crazy reason it carries a status symbol with friends. It is not unusual to hear girls saying to each other in private, "Got it yet? Has it come yet? Now that I have it, what do I do with it? Can I go to physical education?"

They see menses as a symbol of entering womanhood and moving away from "kids" activities. They will often throw away their dolls and begin with the nylons and mini-skirts.

For boys this period is highlighted by nocturnal emissions more commonly known as the "wet dream". Accompanied with this might be the beginning of a masturbatory period. They will find a nice quiet place where they can explore this new excitement. These fantasies will be heightened by the open availability of explicit materials and the imagination of girls in schools who are developing new sensations.

This is going to date me, but I remember when I went through puberty. Years ago if I wanted to see a picture of a naked woman I read National Geographic magazine! After all, there was a copy on our living room coffee table and every time I picked it up to read, my parents were delighted to see me studying the geographical wonders of the world! I remember that on the seventh grade level I would flip through that magazine and come across a naked native woman. I would simply hold it up and study it as a curiosity item only.

When I was in the eighth grade I would look at that magazine and once I found a picture of a naked lady I did not look at it with just curiosity; something had happened to me biologically that even I did not know much about! I now was attracted physically in a new and different way. I would often rip it out and take it to school where I'd show it to my friends and instantly become popular.

On the fifth grade level girls and boys do not look at each other the same way they will on the eighth grade level. At the very time when we want them to put their energies into academics many are spending it attempting to regulate to the explosion of new hormones.

Several studies suggest that about 80% of the boys will be involved in regular masturbation. Only about 20% of the girls will participate in masturbatory activities. My concern is that parents not overreact to this or translate some sort of guilt trip to their youngsters. It would be helpful to get some simple information on this growth stage and leave it around the house where youngsters can get to it when you are not around. They probably won't want to talk about it; but they will be curious and they will attempt to get accurate information as long as it is not embarrassing.

Today kids do not have to read National Geographic to find pictures; they can walk to the convenience store where they are readily available. Parents and churches need to make a serious effort to find ways to educated youngsters on how to understand what is happening and see the dangers particularly in this day and age. In addition to the moral issues, today we need concern ourselves with the life and death issue as it pertains to the AIDS virus. We do know that this is the age level when youngsters might be most vulnerable.

Physically, "frogs" spend an awful lot of time trying to deal with adjustment. They have only so much energy to spend each day to sort it all out. I would like to have some of this energy for academics, but until these problems are sorted, academics might take a back seat for awhile. Wouldn't it be nice if educators were knowledgeable and creative enough to find ways to accommodate for these needs by building constructive activities. Perhaps by giving serious thought to grouping patterns or organizing to insure more home-base guidance activities.

Schools need to work out ways to provide better opportunities to work with parents or perhaps most importantly to build a school mission that is centered around the uniqueness of the early adolescence. It is important to insure that the self-concept is not destroyed over these vulnerable years so that all of this energy becomes our ally rather than fight against it.

THE LEARNING POTENTIAL OF "FROGS"

About age 12 or 13 another developmental change will occur which can cause significant problems in relating with adults. Note that this is a developmental change and youngsters have to wait for it to happen. This is a change that adults won't see happen as they did the physical changes, but once it happens we will know it. We call it a cognitive change which allows our "frogs" to reason differently and to see things they could not previously see. It does not mean that they will wake up on their 13th birthday and display intelligent behavior. It simply means that they will acquire a new potential to reason differently. This potential will depend on adults patiently helping them develop it over these years.

The best way I can describe what happens is to relate how I first noticed the change in my son. He was about 13 years of age. One afternoon he and I were riding in a car on a four-lane highway which circles Boston, Massachusetts. I was driving 65 miles an hour in a 55 mile zone. He suddenly turned toward me and shouted, "DAD!" I was startled and responded by saying, "What is it, Jim!" Then there was this pause as he folded his arms and turned slowly in my direction and said, "Dad, do you realize how fast you are driving this car?" I was obviously embarrassed because after all, I did not want my son to notice that on occasion I break the law! I was able to put this over on him up to this age in his life. But more than that, I was taken back by the new tone in his voice! I had not heard that before. It was a command, not a question! Anyway, he was asking the question so I simply turned and said, "Oh, I'm doing 65 miles per hour!" (as if I didn't know it). He then came right back at me and said, "DAD!" Do you know what the speed limit is on this highway?" Now my ego was hurt and I wanted to attack! This little voice in the back of my head was saying, "Here comes early adolescent behavior, wipe it out now!" Well, he was right, so I kept cool and responded by saying, "Yes Jim, it's 55 miles per hour." He then said, DAD! Do you realize that you are traveling 10 miles over the speed limit"! I handled this one with calm because it at least indicated that he could add and subtract! He continued, "DAD! Don't you care about my life at all! Do you have any idea of how many thousands of people lose their lives every year on our nation's highways who exceed the speed limit! " Now I was beginning to get angry and I responded by saying, "Look Jim, I have no idea how many people are killed every year, you were right I shouldn't have been speeding; I promise I won't ever do it again, so let us just forget it!"

Not being satisfied he continued, "DAD! Any idea what would happen if the front wheel of this car came off doing 65 miles per hour, how many lives you might jeopardize!" He kept on with this for another 10 minutes until I finally got him quiet for about 20 seconds! Then he came back at me and said, "Dad! I've been thinking about this." Once he said that, I knew I was in deep trouble! You see, my son was so easy to deal with before he started TO THINK! Who told him he had a right to start THINKING! Before this all happened he would ask, WHY, and I would simply give him the answer and it was good enough!

Now, a good answer does not exist! Now he wants to analyze my responses! Now it is difficult to finish a sentence without dozens of interruptions!

Once your "frog" moves to this new developmental stage a new capacity will exist to see things that could not be seen before. They will not wake up one morning and be brilliant persons, but will have a new potential to reason differently. Once it begins to happen you will know it because the inquisition will begin!! You might now find yourself having to defend all of your values, rules and directions. They will now have the capacity to see your inconsistencies and once they spot them they will go after your jugular vein!

Try taking a 13-year-old to a ballgame and buying a children's ticket! They will immediately let you know that they are now 13, not 12, and what are you doing buying them a 12-year-old ticket! Or try to order something from the kiddie menu! Yep, they will now have the capacity to see all of those things we used to put over on them. As parents, of course, when this happens we will take the logical approach and sit our "frogs" down and attempt to explain our behavior. Soon after we start, they begin to interrupt and we lose our train of thought. They start thinking faster than us, and we cannot keep our arguments together so we start getting angry and lose everything. It is at this point when we say "GO TO YOUR ROOM!"

Once this "frog" enters this new stage it is

important that we not see his behavior as defiance, but as an opportunity to help develop a new level of thinking. We need to see that this "frog" has at least one person in her life who takes time to help develop this potential. If it is not taught and exercised at the time she is ready this "frog" may never learn to ask the right questions or handle the academic expectations of high school.

Several activities are required to nurture this potential. Providing a climate conducive to questioning is important. Never discourage youngsters from asking questions. It is essential to moving ahead cognitively. It is important to ask questions and to be patient enough to wait for an answer!

We have clocked how long teachers wait for answers and have found that they generally wait two seconds! Wait for an answer and once you get it don't be satisfied with a one word response! Get them to elaborate on their responses such as "How do you know that is true?" or, "How did you come to think about that?" All of these help to build upper level thinking potential. If you can get them to defend their answers you are really doing them a service!

Get them to make decisions about things. Problem centered curricula and discussions in which conclusions must be reached are helpful. Role playing, simulation and drama are a few techniques which work nicely with this problem. Don't feel as if you always have got to give them the answers! I remember a youngster who once said to me, "Dr. Garvin, the reason I don't talk to my parents is because every time we talk they have to win! They always have the answer and could care less what I think!"

They must have opportunities to draw conclusions for themselves and to encourage open-ended discussion where it isn't necessary to come up with the right answer. They have the capacity to think away from us, and will if their curiosity is stimulated.

Schools often exacerbate this problem by expecting learning outcomes not appropriate for the thinking level of this student. The people doing research in this area have shown that about 70% of the eighth graders in this country have not moved to upper level thinking abilities. At least no more than 70% give evidence in school that they can master tasks requiring formal reasoning. Only 24% of the eighth graders show they can comfortably handle tasks requiring formal reasoning.

Let me give you an example of how the two evidence themselves when given a problem. I am going to give a proposition and I want all of my readers to believe it". "ONLY BRAVE PILOTS FLY OVER TALL MOUNTAINS." Now, here is a story; one day a pilot decides to fly over the Swiss Alps. As he approaches the top, for some reason, he flys into a cable car, crashes and dies. That is the end of the story.

Now you are an eighth grader and I ask you, "Given the proposition that 'ONLY BRAVE PILOTS FLY OVER TALL MOUNTAINS' was that pilot brave?" Seventy percent of the eighth graders who are still thinking concretely will respond to that question with a surface response. They might say, "Yep" or "Nope!" or "I don't know?" or "Would you please repeat the question?" Most concrete thinkers do not give elaborate answers because they do not think about alternatives when given a problem. Many of them watch the teacher perform and not think until they are put on the spot. When asked to elaborate they generally give reference to some event they experienced in life. Some will be very stubborn and will take a point of view and not open themselves to alternatives even though their position is obviously wrong!

In parenting this behavior drives us nuts! They won't see the obvious just because it is not their viewpoint. Concrete learners are like this and they represent about 70% of the eighth graders. Twenty-four percent of these youngsters respond differently. These are the youngsters who move ahead developmentally and are fortunate to be around people who encourage them to think differently. In response to this proposition they say, "Wait a minute, I can't answer that question, you haven't given me enough information yet!" Because this youngster has the ability to think differently he starts thinking along with the teacher as the problem is presented.

When the teacher finishes, this youngster will have a new set of questions to ask because he analyzed the problem as it was described! He might continue in his response by saying , "I can't answer this yet because I need to know more about the pilot; I need to know more about the weather; what about the condition of the plane?" This youngster will ask these questions because he can see alternatives, he can reason about new things, things that are not inherent in the original story.

About 5% of the youngsters who hear this story will respond in a seemingly ridiculous fashion by saying, "What color was the cable car?" These are youngsters who have not yet reached the level of concrete reasoning and cannot see how parts of the story make a whole. They often get preoccupied with one aspect and develop it apart from the rest of the story.

Given this problem, it is a major concern of mine that many of the textbooks written for early adolescents are filled with upper level or abstract terminology and expectations which very few of these youngsters give evidence they can do! It is perhaps most evident in math word problems. Some of these problems have vocabulary that is very abstract making it even more difficult to do the thinking required to work out the answer!

I remember one of my children during the sixth grade had a reading program that required learning the definition to lots of vocabulary words every night. Most of these words were abstract, so my "frog" was not able to do the kind of thinking it required so he resorted to a meaningless memorization solution. Consequently, having memorized the definition, passing a vocabulary test was easy. This process consequence was not to understand context and meaning; therefore the word was not appreciated and became counterproductive in the reading from which the word was abstracted. Both the words and the story were abstract so this "frog" learned how to lose interest in reading school assigned materials.

Knowing that the vast majority of these eighth grade "frogs" are thinking concretely I am saddened by the indiscriminate manner some teachers select curriculum and develop grouping patterns. For example, we have a fetish in this country that youngsters are retarded if they cannot do algebra by the eighth grade. I remind you that unless your "frog" can do upper level thinking he will not be able to figure out algebraic equations. To do algebra one must be able to see something that is not concrete.

It requires converting symbols from something not present!

Numbers are fine because they are concrete, but let a teacher put up brackets or symbols and all of a sudden many of these "frogs" are in trouble. This requires another level of thinking for which either they haven't yet matured developmentally, or have, but have not had instruction to practice it sufficiently.

In many schools I have visited, as many as 44% of the youngsters are in algebra classes when no more than half have matured to that required level of thinking. Here is what can happen; let us say that your daughter is in this algebra class and she has not yet matured to do this required level of thinking. She might even have a high I.Q. because I.Q. doesn't always tell us if a youngster can do upper level thinking. We often get into serious trouble with this one because if a youngster has a high I.Q. chances are that this youngster will end up in upper level classes which will most likely require upper level thinking which hasn't yet been attained! The result, a good possibility that the experience becomes counterproductive and the youngster ends up hating it.

In this algebra class if this "frog" cannot draw the connections she will probably take lots of notes (a good concrete operation) and proceed home to get help from Mom and Dad. If Mom and Dad can do upper level thinking perhaps they will be of some help. This is not likely in many families because they never understood the thinking required for these equations themselves.

Only 55% of the adults in this country give evidence they can do upper level thinking! Many have an Archie Bunker lifestyle where they work at non-thinking tasks all day, come home and watch TV until bedtime. They cannot help this youngster because they haven't practiced the thinking required to see the problem themselves! Then this "frog" will probably call a friend hoping she has figured it out. If she has, she will explain it by breaking it down into pieces so it can be memorized. Then this little girl will go to her math class the next day, sit in the back and pray that the teacher will not call on her. Then she will begin to play the game of school.

Most students learn the game of school on the middle level out of frustration and as a survival technique. She will memorize everything hoping that it will someday make sense! She will beg, borrow, steal, or hold up kids on the way to school to copy work. She will get the teacher to give answers, anything to better understand something she is not yet mature enough to understand. If this little girl predicts properly, she might pass that subject, but if she passes not understanding the concepts of algebra, do not be surprised if she avoids algebra like the plague the rest of her life!

It is tragic because once she moves ahead cognitively in her thinking and is capable of doing algebra she will be convinced she cannot, simply because we have chosen to assign this class without knowing if her age-learner characteristics match the subject. It is not that we shouldn't teach algebra at the eighth grade level, but it does mean we need to find ways to identify what kind of thinking is required and insure that youngsters can do it. If they cannot then we had better service them by offering a class that teaches and practices the thinking before expecting them to accomplish tasks that require it.

In English, on the eighth grade level "frogs" are generally working on literature. "Frogs" need to learn to respect good literature and more importantly learn to develop good attitudes about the value of good literature. I suggest that in some of these eighth grade classes we teach the opposite because of the assumptions we make about the thinking capacity of these youngsters and the mismatch that occurs when we assign things to read that require upper level thinking.

It may not be unusual for an eighth grade teacher to expect a youngster to find symbolism or imagery or metaphor in a piece of literature. Keep in mind that all of these expectations require that a youngster has moved ahead in thinking to see something that is not concrete. This requires being able to see something not present, something that will require inference and putting together several things to form conclusions. All of these youngsters will be able to learn a definition of all three and probably will convince the classroom teacher that this is enough to find it in a story.

Definition is a concrete level exercise which most youngsters on the eighth grade level can perform. But, to find it in a story requires a completely different kind of thinking that most "frogs" do not attain because it must be taught and practiced with connections to concrete examples. When a simple assumption is made that students can do it because they are NOW EIGHTH GRADERS, those who cannot begin to play the game of school to avoid failure or punitive discipline. They will first underline everything in the book!! On the way home, if they can afford it, they will soon learn the value of CLIFF NOTES!!! Yes, CLIFF will now become the cure-all because with CLIFF you do not have to think, you simply memorize the outline which in most cases will satisfy most teachers.

I am amazed at how many of my college students live and die by Cliff Notes. They have learned that thinking is not necessary and, after all, playing the game has worked for them for so many years! This literature teacher may very well turn off many "frogs" to read another piece of literature again! Literature is important to teach "frogs" but abstract assignments will require that first of all a teacher help students to practice how to do the thinking required. If youngsters complete eighth grade hating this sort of reading they will be lost in high school where the reading requires an even higher level of thinking.

The point here is that teachers need to be less concerned with the content and more concerned with teaching the basic thinking skills required to understand the content! There are several good tests on the market to test where students are cognitively. They need to be purchased and used in determining curriculum, methodology and grouping patterns.

Parents should be familiar with reading assignments given to their "frogs". If they have trouble understanding, we must find ways to relate it to situations they understand. It will take prodding them into the thinking level required to do the assignment. This will mean that parents must take a more active role in knowing what schools are expecting.

If our "frogs" are trying and cannot seem to draw the inferences then we need to consider taking them out of these classes until we are sure they are ready for the level of thinking required. Above all we must not set them up for failure by expecting them to do something that just happens to be in the curriculum but has not taken into consideration whether or not our child has reached the cognitive thinking level required. Literature is one of those subjects in which I see the reality of this occurring frequently.

In science we learned that I.P.S. (Individually Prescribed Science) was a dismal failure because it required upper level thinking which very few seventh graders could perform. It was eventually moved to the ninth grade where it is meeting with better success. Lab experiences can be useful because they are "hands-on", concrete ways to break down and experience learning. However, if the text describes the task in abstract terms, the student will do the lab wrong.

All teachers need to be teachers of reading simply because all reading assignments must be within the capacity of age-learner characteristics. Teachers and parents need to check for abstract terms and translate them in concrete terms for the 70% who need it. Math is closely connected with science and again it is important to understand that the kind of math required must be concrete or practice in the new form of thinking will be necessary.

In social studies there are those who really think "frogs" are capable of inductive and deductive reasoning. They might have the capacity to learn but only 24% give any evidence they can actually do it at the eighth grade level. Yet there are major curriculums that require inductive and deductive reasoning to pass a social studies course. Some opt to be placed in lower-tracked classes. Worst of all, some give up and become docile.

My favorite eighth grade teacher was a history teacher. I will never forget her as long as I live. She was in her sixties and near to her retirement. Every day she would have all sorts of things on the board, mostly timelines or completed outlines. She always had every space of her room filled with exciting pictures depicting history. She looked busy all the time. Her hands were always marked with blue ink, her clothes constantly had chalk marks on them from leaning against the board.

I used to think that this teacher had to be up preparing all night just for our class. She had so many activities prepared to explain to us the lessons for each day. I know now why I was a straight "A" student in her class! Everything she prepared was so concrete. A concrete learner needs lots of trees before seeing the forest. An abstract learner can see the forest right away! I needed trees because I was one of those who hadn't been taught how to do formal thinking.

Interestingly enough, about half way through this eighth grade experience the principal decided to remove me from this class because I was doing so well. He marched me down the corridor to another history class named "PROBLEMS OF DEMO-CRACY". I still remember that because what I was about to experience was not productive. As I entered the class I noticed 12 students in a circle around this teacher who was pontificating on all of the major constructs of democracy! I thought I was a pretty good student because in the other class I was quite productive and successful.

I was introduced to the teacher as an excellent student which to the teacher was interpreted to mean I was prepared for his curriculum and abstract instructional techniques. It didn't take me long to discover that I had no idea what this teacher was talking about! He kept throwing questions at me that I couldn't understand which led to embarrassment and eventual failure. I remember asking the principal if I could return to the class where I was successful and his response was, "You're too smart for that class, you must stay here, it will be good for you." I eventually failed and guess what kind of teachers I avoided in high school? Anyone who wanted me to think!!! The mistake people make is assuming when a student is performing well in one class that it means they can do the same in all classes. The first teacher I had knew how to work with concrete learners and was slowly helping them to learn how to think about what she had worked hard to make practical! The other teachers in the school did not like her because they thought she was "spoon feeding us". What the other teachers did not know is that this teacher was probably the most effective teacher in the school because she was "pitching the ball where kids could hit it!"

Remember I mentioned that this teacher had lots of pictures on her walls? What an exciting learning climate she created! I wonder what happens when kids move to the junior high? In some of them the only thing you see on the walls is a half portrait of George Washington! It is amazing when you stop to think about it. Children arrive from elementary schools where they experience classrooms alive with color and illustration. What a downer experience to enter this large building called the junior high that has lost all excitement of creative illustrations for a new image of academic halls of wisdom! My eighth grade teacher was different in this respect because she didn't really care what others thought about her room; she knew whatever these pictures did, they worked to make "frogs" more excited about history.

There is a great deal of research on what is called
MODALITY PREFERENCE. MODALITIES are
vehicles we use to process information. We all do
this either auditorially (hearing), visually (seeing) or
kinesthetically (hands on). All are necessary for
effective learning, but most "frogs" have a biological
preference which when matched allows for better
processing, longer concentration and consequently
better learning. The data seems to suggest that
only 20% of these "frogs" learn best when teachers
just talk! Unfortunately, on the seventh and eighth
grade levels a good proportion of instruction comes
through teachers who lecture! About 45% of "frogs"
are visual and learn best from teachers who have
lots of pictures, or frequently use media.

The history teacher I liked really knew what she
was doing because not only did she teach within my
cognitive level, she also provided instruction on a
modality level which I had greater strength to
understand! About 35% of these "frogs" are
kinesthetic, which means that these youngsters
work well when given hands-on tasks to perform.

Looking at this profile it becomes obvious that
teachers who expect to be successful with these
"frogs" are going to be those whose methodology is
primarily visual and kinesthetic! It is no surprise
that the teachers in the applied and fine arts areas
are so well-liked. These teachers seldom waste time
talking. They keep students doing things which
brings high student interest because it matches
modality preference. In these areas if students
finish a piece of art or build a bookcase, they will
prize and cherish it for life. Wouldn't it be nice to
say the same about a math paper or an essay?
Teachers in arts naturally produce climates that
match the modality preferences of "frogs".

Students often signal their modality preference. Those who respond to learning by saying, "I hear you", are probably auditory because this is how they are processing the situation. Then there are those who might respond by saying, "Now I see it!" These are most likely visual learners. Visual learners are also doodlers. They need to see it, so while the teacher is talking away they almost unconsciously move into a doodling activity that puts thoughts into pictures.

Then there are those who learn best by doing, who might respond by saying, "That's dynamite!" or, "That's powerful!" These are "frogs" who see it in terms of action. It is interesting that elementary school students not only have several options to learning but much of their day is spent with visual and active learning activities. Once they enter the middle level school such options are replaced by an organized, fixed day with limited time periods and increased curriculum expectations.

The result is that students who need to continue learning patterns developed on the elementary school level are suddenly expected to put aside these biological preferences and conform to high school expectations. The result is often meaningless experiences and a heightened dislike for learning. The more they sit and listen, the less they see and do, the more probability they will lose interest and the less prepared they will be for future expectations.

Studies show that most girls are auditory-visual while boys are visual-kinesthetic. If you give a boy and a girl a textbook to read on the eighth grade level, most girls will take the time to read the first paragraph but boys will immediately start looking for pictures. Boys are more visual! I have often been asked why boys can sit in front of a computer for hours. The answer is probably quite clear. A computer provides a visual stimulus and the keyboard is kinesthetic (hands on) which is a good modality match for most boys.

I have been involved in an interesting experiment over the past three years. I have been visiting shopping malls to watch early adolescent behavior. The place I have shown most attention is in the arcades. I have watched "frogs" at those machines. I have learned that boys play the machines twice that of girls. They are better than girls (probably because they play them more). They are better than their parents because their parents show little patience and they do not like to lose.

I have tracked down ten of these "frogs" who are the champions. Their names are up on the machines as having recorded the highest scores. After interviewing them I discovered something very interesting. Of the ten I interviewed, nine were boys and eight were classified as "at risk" students in school! What does all of this mean? Mastering these machines requires a great deal of intellectual and motor talent. Kids make more decisions in two minutes of working these machines than they will make all day in school. They need to be able to read directions, to act quickly, make split second judgments and anticipate future encounters. Yet these boys who could master all of these things in the arcade mall did not view school as important enough to transfer the skills to the learning process.

Maybe if we spent more time trying to learn what these machines do to attract attention we might be better able to help these kids in school. Maybe these machines are a better modality match bringing out a natural human potential. But then again, bringing these things to school to replace the hours of sitting and listening to boring lectures would be quite radical wouldn't it?

Parents need to know how to help their "frogs" understand difficult concepts by using whatever might be the dominate modality preference. Both learning and correction are ineffective unless we use more visual examples or action experiences to explain our instruction. The more they do with us or the more we draw examples from their lives, the better they understand difficult concepts. The more personal it is, the more it will be heard and the greater concentration we can expect. It is here where parents have an advantage over teachers because we know more about our "frogs" from which to draw examples. I for one am pleased to see computer companies developing software that breaks down difficult school concepts into visual patterns.

Another area where "frogs" begin to lose it in school is related to what neurologists call hemispheric dominance. The human brain has two sides. The left side deals with language, deadlines, order, sequence and details. The right hemisphere is the non-language side of the brain which deals with intuition, hunches and "gut" feelings. Persons with dominance in the left side would never write a check from the checkbook unless everything has been balanced first! They are not comfortable sitting at a desk unless everything is in place. They might not make a decision unless they are sure that all the data is in first! This is just the way they approach problems because it represents a biological preference.

The person who is dominant in the right hemisphere approaches things quite differently.

Such individuals write checks because they have a hunch there is enough money in the bank! They add up the checkbook to the nearest hundred! If I had a group of people in a room I could probably demonstrate the problem by setting up the following situation.

I would put all of the people who are dominant in the left hemisphere on one side of the room and those who are dominant in the right on the other side. Then I would give them a task to perform and send them out of the room for 15 minutes to solve it and plan a presentation. After 15 minutes those who approached the problem from the left hemisphere will return right on time and have a spokesperson and probably several flow charts! Those in the group that approaches the problem from the right hemisphere will not be back. You will have to go get them, since they simply do not respect deadlines!

Once both groups return and give their presentations they will probably dislike each other's techniques. The right hemispheric people will be bored silly as they gaze upon all those facts and flow charts! The left hemispheric people will be angry with the right hemispheric people's presentation because they will be "conceptual" or "holistic". Yet both took the assignment and worked hard on it. Hemispheric dominance tells us how we approach problems. After four seconds both hemispheres are working, but it is important to know how "frogs" approach problems because we could miss their dominance and turn them off before we get started.

It has been estimated that 70% of all instruction in school is geared to the left hemisphere. If this is true then what happens to the youngster who is more dominant in the right (mostly boys)? Studies have shown that when boys and girls start school perhaps girls are a year to a year and half ahead of boys in left hemispheric development. If this is true then girls will have a clear advantage because most of what will be taught will center around language and organization. The result of ignoring this situation is that when these "frogs" get to the eighth grade level there will be a 10-1 ratio of boys to girls in remedial reading classes. Ninety-five percent of the hyperactives will be boys, not girls!

Those who are fortunate enough to be dominant in the left hemisphere will fit nicely into the patterns established in school for success. The others might become docile, or act out to prevent learning or maybe even just drop out of school. On the early adolescent level " frogs" who are not a match step out, in high school they will drop out.

Another interesting aspect of this is that some studies show that many of the gifted and talented students are more dominant in the right hemisphere although the school pattern does not lend itself to that dominance. This happens because the giftedness allows them to do more independent work which strengthens opportunities to release their human learning potential. If you are classified as "gifted" you have a better chance to find a match of biological potential to learning expectations. Others simply have to find a way to adapt.

Students who are dominant in the left hemisphere will love organized teachers. They love to take notes or follow outlines, even if they don't understand them! As long as they are engaged in an organized instruction pattern their organism is satisfied. They are patient and have faith that the end result will lead to understanding. Students who are dominate in the right hemisphere do not have the patience to take lots of notes or stick to outlines. These students need to see things holistically. They learn best when teachers put the details into stories to hold their attention, so when timelines are given, they can see where they are going.

When teachers explain at the outset what they hope to do so students can keep the master-plan in mind as they receive details, these students learn best by not knowing what it is happening. When teachers ignore one or the other it is done at the peril of the student. Teachers need to keep in mind that both hemispheres are necessary to do formal thinking. Perhaps the reason we evidence only 24% able to do it at the eighth grade is because we do not give enough attention to the right hemisphere.

We often slip into teaching methods in which we feel comfortable and which satisfy our learning style. Often students are not given the luxury of choosing how they will learn in the classroom. To a great extent teachers make that choice. Those students who have styles that match the teacher will learn best. Teachers must find ways to convey material in alternative ways that might help students process it in ways they learn best.

If a "frog" goes to this middle level school and has a teacher who has selected a curriculum that is abstract when he has not yet developed thinking levels to understand it or has teaching methods which require higher thinking levels than attained, that is one strike against him. If this same teacher talks all day when he processes material better visually or kinesthetically, that is two strikes against him. Then, if most of the instruction is geared to the left hemisphere when he is dominant in the right, that is three strikes against him. For this student to like school, much less learn anything, is marginal at most! I have a strange feeling that many of the youngsters in resource rooms across the country are not there because they have learning difficulties. They are there out of survival to escape the mismatch of learning styles in the regular classrooms. Resource room teachers take the time to identify learning styles before proceeding with instruction.

Parents need to insure that teachers are trained to test and group according to these learning styles. There are tests on the market that parents can give to help them know how to use these styles in settling home issues. Often parents assume that their children have the same learning style when this is possibly not true.

Explaining rules, teaching responsibility, understanding correction might go right past the youngster unless it is delivered where the youngster can understand it. I have heard some parents trying to sound "professional" or "esoteric" to their children only to draw a blank response. Parents need to leave the "professional jargon" for their world and work hard at breaking down conversation to the concrete levels of their "frogs".

THE STRESS OF
BEING A 'FROG"

Last year I remember one day when I had to fulfill a speaking engagement in Connecticut. I started the day with a series of successful events. I had a good breakfast with my family, made it to my first class with plenty of time to spare, had a good exchange with my students and overall felt pretty good. These successful events built my ego strength to a high level. Consequently, my ability to handle stress was increased sizably. I remember how good I felt as I started on the trip. I knew it would take me about three hours with clear, written directions from the school's principal. As I left Gordon College I was feeling great, my stress level was low and my ego strength high.

About an hour along the way I ran into some traffic resulting from a car accident. As I sat in line waiting for the traffic to move I started looking at the clock. I still had ample time to comfortably make it to the school, so, I continued to be relaxed. Finally the traffic started moving again and somehow I felt that whatever stress I had gathered was still well under control.

About 30 minutes later I ran into another traffic accident. This time it was an 18-wheeler that had jackknifed in the middle of the highway blocking everything. Now I really started to worry because this situation looked like it would bring a much longer delay than the previous one. I did not panic because I had some pretty good ego strength from which to draw upon to handle the stress that was now beginning to develop. As I sat and waited, I kept looking at my watch and the more I did, the more I was reminded that I was running out of time. The stress was now beginning to eat away at the ego strength. The traffic started to move again and my ego was once again in charge.

As I arrived in the city where the school is located, I looked at my watch again and saw that I was just going to make it. I quickly looked at the directions I had been given and carefully followed them only to find that they were wrong. Now I'm lost, I'm late and in the middle of nowhere! Then I made the mistake of looking at my fuel gauge only to see that I was sitting on empty!!! What now? Do I stop and phone the principal to tell him I am lost or do I keep going to make the best use of time? Do I stop and get gas or do I chance it?

Now the ego strength I left with has run its course and the stress is about to take over. I am now unable to think clearly, much less able to make the right decision. Now I am angry at myself and at the principal for giving me poor directions. Here I am about to address a staff of teachers, and I am out of control because I had reached my stress level.

As I moved along lost, I saw a telephone repairman. He gave me directions to the school which was ten minutes away! I started to think about how angry this group of teachers must be sitting and waiting for my arrival. I thought of how angry the principal must be not knowing where I am! My next move is to begin making up some excuses so that when I arrive I can smooth things over! More stress developed as I wondered if the excuses would work?

I finally pulled up to the school about 20 minutes late. I then saw the principal dash out of the front door heading towards my car with this seemingly disappointed look on his face. Being completely out of control I opened the door of my car ready to give what I thought to be a forgiving excuse for being so late. About to open my mouth, this principal put his arm around my shoulder and immediately started to tell me how excited everyone is to have me at his school!

Wow!! My ego was regenerated as he went on to tell me that things were hectic for his staff all day and they had to move everything back an hour and went on to apologize for not being able to contact me about it! Let me tell you, my stress level was lowered immediately and with it a comfortable feeling that led to a confident successful presentation to that staff of teachers.

Stress often causes irrational behavior. The best cure for stress is to replace it with ego strength. Over these vulnerable early adolescent years "frogs" might encounter disappointments at a more rapid pace than any other period of life. One only has to look at what is happening to this age level to see the signs of stress. These signs are never pretty and we always hope that they affect someone else's "frog", but the intensity of expectations in this world makes all of them susceptible. Look with me for a minute at some of the things that are happening to teens today that are signs of unmanageable stress . . .

Suicide is one of the leading causes of deaths for early adolescents. There is one attempt every 32 seconds. More girls attempt suicide than boys but more boys actually complete the act. Thirty two percent of these suicides occur either one hour before school, during school or one hour after school. Somehow what happens in school is so stressful that these youngsters perceive they can no longer deal with life.

There are many reasons for this behavior, but when one looks carefully into it the results are the same, a fractured self esteem, no ego strength, at least not enough to manage the stress.

One of the reasons these youngsters follow this awful course of action centers around feelings of despair. Some no longer want to try because whatever source of strength they perceived is no longer there or at least is no longer dependable. Perhaps the place where this is most telling is in the developing surge of broken families. Forty percent of the "frogs" in grades 6, 7 and 8 have only one parent at home! This does not necessarily mean that the single-parent situation is terminal because we know many youngsters are better off in a strong single parent situation than an abusive, weak, two-parent situation. However, the process often involved in divorce and separation creates difficult adjustments which make them feel that the security once provided by the home is gone and that they can no longer handle the pressures of life. Some even blame themselves for the separation of their parents creating more guilt that produces additional stress. They often put energies into trying to put Mom and Dad back together causing a scenario of more failure, more disappointment, more despair and alienation.

Ninety percent of the single parents are working all day which puts additional pressure on relationships. Some who have studied this problem have shown a direct correlation of acting out in school and academic failure related to the pressure of the fractured family. When more failure occurs, acting out inevitably results in punitive discipline seldom conducive to ego strength. Consequently this make the youngster more vulnerable to suicide.

Another reason that seems to be surfacing regarding this sudden increase in suicide centers around a group of "frogs" who simply give up! They are youngsters who have worked endlessly to satisfy significant others, but for some reason have never quite made the grade. Sadly, many of these "frogs" are in the "gifted and talented" category. These youngsters are blessed with the talent to achieve but sometimes have parents who see them only as achievers! Many of these youngsters after a season simply get the message that their acceptance is contingent on achieving higher and higher levels which are never really attainable. After a time these youngsters begin to wonder if anyone cares about the rest of their lives. They simply get tired. The stress becomes too much and the ego strength too little so they begin a pattern of behaviors which strikes out at those who have failed them.

When one studies anorexia or bulimia in the 10-14 age group it becomes apparent that most are girls from affluent families and the vast majority of them are gifted and talented. It is their way of moving to something they can control that may eventually become terminated in a dreadful ending.

We need to have good gifted and talented programs in our schools, but the minute they produce an outcome of unmanageable stress they should be examined and changed. Above all, we need to find ways to attend to the whole child not just from the shoulders up!

In my region of the country, six "frogs" have committed suicide during this past school year. In three of the cases youngsters came to school with a gun and held hostages. Two of these youngsters shot their hostage before turning the gun on themselves. In examining these cases I learned that when this was happening the principals could not find one faculty member who knew these youngsters well enough to talk them out of this behavior, much less knew them well enough to have spotted the symptoms before it happened!

In many of our middle level schools no provisions are made in the daily schedule to provide youngsters with opportunities to get to know an adult well enough to find ego support. Many of these schools are organized in such a way that there is a 5-10 minute homeroom in which most of the time is spent in taking attendance and reading daily announcements!

These youngsters are released to attend several classes in which teachers only see students once each day centered around an area of instruction not for the sake of building good advisor/advisee relationships. Consequently, many youngsters simply fall between the cracks and whatever problems might exist in their lives over these critical years are left for the youngsters to resolve.

When a student brings a gun to school and does something disastrous, then and only then do we stop the process long enough to grieve, but hardly never to correct the problem in the system which could have prevented it to begin with. Even guidance counselors cannot do the job because in most systems we only place one counselor for every 300 students. I suggest that once you get to know the complications of this age level you will understand that this is far from adequate.

Parents ought to demand that middle level schools provide a home base of teachers for students, who can come to know them well enough to identify when stress needs attending to. I have observed schools that have organized to the interdisciplinary team approach designed to provide good advisor/advisee possibilities. Teachers come to know a small group of students from which to provide for their everchanging developmental needs. This organization increases the probability of being sensitive to problems of despair and disappointment. These schools are committed philosophically to a child-centered approach and to providing a climate conducive to build good mental health, without which, lasting learning will not occur anyway.

Beyond suicide, there are other signs of stress in early adolescents. The largest group of runaways are "frogs" aged 13. These are youngsters searching for someone to help them understand themselves. These are youngsters who unfortunately will meet charlatans who will tell them that they need to join cults or to become part of groups designed to turn them against the world. Both represent a horrendous way to waste human potential.

People who cannot handle stress often run. The running is a symptom of a person who does not see himself as worthwhile or loved or forgiven or adequate. It is often a sign that self esteem has been destroyed and they become like an open nerve ready to be manipulated by those in our society who prey on using others for their own advantage. One only needs to visit a bus station or an airport to see hundreds of these "frogs" looking out the window wishing they could be on the plane or bus to get away from the unmanageable stress in their lives.

Two years ago I remember stopping to pick up a youngster who was hitchhiking. he held in his hand a sign which read "PLEASE TAKE ME ANYWHERE, BUT GET ME OUT OF HERE!" He was running away from people who had destroyed his self esteem and was willing to try anything else. I suggest that many hundreds of these youngsters do this every day without holding a sign, but nevertheless with the same intention.

There will be a 26% increase in hard drug use over grades 6-9. There will be a 29% increase in alcohol use. In my state one out of every ten "frogs" will have a police record before the age of 14. I suggest these are serious signs of stress. For the most part these youngsters are crying out for help!

I have worked with many youngsters who have been on drugs and I concluded that most of these youngsters have one basic problem-their self esteem is destroyed. They could care less about what happens to themselves, or what happens around them! They then collect with others who are experiencing the same thing and the habit becomes the glue that joins them together. It helps them run away and forget about the worthless feelings they have about themselves.

I am concerned about the direction this country seems to be taking in demanding more at an earlier age, insuring more stress for these youngsters. Educators are obsessed with raising achievement scores and getting youngsters to satisfy the high school demands at an earlier age. I see some elementary schools becoming departmentalized and adopting a tracking system. I see little or no attention on the part of State education officials to recognize or encourage teacher preparation to work with these kids. I see some states opting for more content-centered, five year teacher preparation programs which will inevitably lead to more rigorous academic programs in the middle grades bringing perhaps more of the mindset that these kids need to grow up faster.

We must demand that adults who are going to work with "frogs" be people who are concerned about mental health, about providing ego strength, and about knowing the complications of this critical level of development. We must provide "frogs" with opportunities to explore and create and think about who they are and what they can be. "Frogs" must have mentors who themselves have good mental health and value it enough to reproduce it in their students.

I am concerned about the responsibility level of network television and the media. Television is the number one curriculum for early adolescents. Many are addicted to watching television which often becomes a form of escape or denial. Early adolescents watch 1,500 hours of television by the age of 15 compared to 1,100 hours in school.

Television often produces the image that everything is going to be fine, all that is necessary is to buy this or that or have this or that. "Frogs" watch it and get messages that success in life is directly related to material well-being. Some will translate this into the message that wealth is the only answer to a successful life. They will soon come to believe that education is important only as a vehicle to make money and become rich.

Other network programs transfer messages that adults are idiots and cannot be trusted. Many of the situation comedies which portray young adolescents show parents as bungling idiots who end up week after week having their problems solved by their adolescent. The messages are clearly not realistic but who cares as long as kids watch it and their parents buy the products they advertise . . . even if it distorts the relationship between the role of parents and that of children.

Television is such a powerful media, it is a shame that we have not learned how to use it to assist kids as they grow and adjust to the many problems adults have handed them in this age. Screening the trash and being selective of what our children watch is absolutely necessary.

Early adolescents need help in sorting out the messages and guidance in seeing the trappings. We need to learn how to replace television with wholesome positive experiences. We need to recapture the time when we went places together, got involved in activities together, participated in projects together, did things for others together.

Building good mental health requires that we feel the need to be part of a community. We need to know that we belong and are important and appreciated. Those activities which move us away from community participation must be eliminated and replaced with active, constructive events. Kids who spend the day watching television, or hiding in the back of the class, or running away, unfortunately, have never experienced the good feeling of community. Somehow they were never included, or if they were they were somehow told that they didn't fit.

Some of these "frogs" have watched their home community break up and they need other positive communities to hold them up as they struggle to understand and rebuild. Churches, schools and community groups need to make this a top priority.

We only need to see how many thousands of kids we lose every day to cults which attract "frogs" who are simply looking to find the community experiences they never had, or had, but didn't last.

Studies show that it is not the message of these cults that attracts adolescents, it is the closeness, warmth, caring and family and community. We must do a better job than these potentially destructive groups by rethinking our priorities and building positive community experiences through the schools every day.

Yes, youngsters who are 11-14 are like "frogs". We need to understand more of what they experience over these years so we as adults can stop blaming ourselves for their behavior and put our energies into building positive experiences designed to accommodate these unique behaviors. Keep in mind that adults who have the patience and can kiss these "frogs" on a regular basis will make all the difference in the world.

Parents need to tell their "frogs" they love them every day. Don't expect a magnificent response. Just do it because we know that it is perhaps the most powerful source of strength "frogs" have. They don't need adults in their lives who make love contingent on something. They don't need a bonus love that is given as they fulfill the ideal! They need to know through all of this awkward behavior, as difficult as it may be, they are still loved.

As they learn to conceptualize they come to accept what is important through the way it has shaped the adults teaching them. If adults scream and yell and lose control, "frogs" learn quickly not to listen. "Frogs" look carefully at the life styles of adults and often what we say speaks so loud that they cannot hear what we say. We need to understand that over these years we must reevlauate our own lives to insure that we project models that youngsters see are worth emulating. We must provide good models in our schools, churches and community organizations. We must see to it that these youngsters have access to good people who respect the quality of human life through advisor/advisee experiences.

These years come and go very quickly, we only have them for such a short time. These years are critical to this passage from being a child to facing the adult world. While we have them in this time of passage we must not destroy their self-concept. We must help them see that they are special and work hard to identify their given human potential and see to it that they are in the right place and with the right people who can help them recognize and release their potential in a manner that enhances human life itself.

BIBLIOGRAPHY

BOOKS FOR TEENS, PRE-TEENS
AND THEIR PARENTS

In response to many requests from parents, here is a list of books about human sexuality for teenagers, and a few for parents.

FOR PRE-TEENS:

"Love and Sex and Growing Up", by Eric W. Johnson and Corrine Johnson (J.B. Lippincott. Distributed by Harper and Row, and Bantam).

"Making Sense of Sex: The New Facts About Sex and Love for Young People", by Helen Singer Kaplan (Simon and Schuster).

"What's Happening to ME?" by Peter Mayle (Lyle Stuart) Good information on how the body changes.

FOR EARLY TEENS:

"The Teenage Survival Book", by Sol Gordon (Times Books). A lively, illustrated paperback for kids who don't like to read.

"You Would If You Loved Me", by Sol Gordon (Bantam). The lines kids use to pressure each other for sex.

"Sex With Love: A Guide For Young People," by Elenor Hamilton (Bacon Press). Suggestions about how to be loving without intercourse.

"Love and Sex in Plain Language," by Eric W. Johnson (J.B. Lippincott, distributed by Harper and Row, and Bantam). Basic facts and personal responsibility.

"Growing Up With Sex: A Guide For Early Teens," by Richard F. Hettlinger (Continuum Publishing Co.) Sex education with special reference to Christian values.

"Boys and Sex", by Wardell B. Pomeroy (Dell). Facts and feelings of male sexuality.

"Girls and Sex." The same thing for girls.

OLDER TEENS:

"Changing Bodies, Changing Lives," by Ruth Bell (Random House). The most comprehensive book for teens.

"The Teenage Body Book," by Kathy McCoy and Charles Wibbelsman (Simon and Schuster). How a rapidly maturing body affects your life.

"Commonsense Sex," by Ronald Mazur (Beacon Press). Sexuality discussed in a liberal religous context.

"What Are You Using? A Birth Control Guide For Teenagers," by Andres Balis (dial)

SPECIAL TOPICS:

"Am I Parent Material?" A pamphlet available form the National Alliance for Optional Parenthood, 1439 Rhode Isalnd Ave., N.W. Washington, D.C. 20005.

"STD: A Commonsense Guide," by Maria Corsare and Carole Korzenlowsky (St. Martin's Press). The facts about veneral disease.

"A Way of Love, a Way of Life: A Young person's Introduction to What It Means To Be Gay," by Frances Hanckel and John Cunningham (Lothrop, Lee and Shepard).

FOR PARENTS:

"The Family Book About Sexuality," by Mary S. Calderone and Eric W. Johnson (Harper and Row).

"How to Talk to your Teenager About Something That's Not Easy to Talk About." Pamphlet available (50 cents) from Planned Parenthood of America, Inc., 810 Seventh Ave., New York, NY 10019

"Sex And The American Teenager: A Guide For Parents," by Murray Kappelman (Readers Digest Press).

"The Best Kept Secret: Sexual Abuse of Children," by Florence Rush (McGraw Hill). How to help kids avoid abuse and harassment.

"A Family Matter: A Parent's Guide to Homosexuality, " by Charles Silverstein. A doctor's advice about how to accept a child's homosexuality.

ABOUT THE AUTHOR

Jim Garvin has had a long career working with early adolescents. He has taught grades 7, 8 & 9, directed a summer camp for 1600 early adolescents, developed and chaired a middle school teacher education program. His career was further distinguished by serving on state department teacher education advisory committees and accepting an assignment with the National Commission on Excellence in which he visited exemplary middle schools throughout the country. He is former Executive Director of the New England League of Middle Schools and past President of the National Middle School Association.

Jim has received many honors for his outstanding contributions to middle level education. These include the Outstanding Educator Award for the Massachusetts and Connecticut Principals Association, the President's Award from the National Middle School Association and the Outstanding Faculty Member Award from Gordon College.

Jim is in great demand as a lecturer and consultant to middle level schools and parent groups. He has presented at national conferences and served on many middle level school advisory committees. He has conducted hundreds of in service workshops for teachers, parents and human service people.

He has published over 75 articles in major publications, has contributed to 15 monographs and authored three books.

Jim resides with his wife Jo-Ann, and their daughter, Hope. He attributes a great deal of his expertise to his three older children, Debijoy, Faith and Jim II, who taught him how to deal with early adolescence.